FOOD LOVERS

CHOCOLATE

FOOD LOVERS
CHOCOLATE

RECIPES SELECTED BY ALEKSANDRA MALYSKA

Trans
Atlantic
Press

All recipes serve four people,
unless otherwise indicated.

For best results when cooking the recipes in this book, buy fresh ingredients and follow the instructions carefully. Make sure that everything is properly cooked through before serving, particularly any meat and shellfish, and note that as a general rule vulnerable groups such as the very young, elderly people, pregnant women, convalescents and anyone suffering from an illness should avoid dishes that contain raw or lightly cooked eggs.

For all recipes, quantities are given in standard U.S. cups and imperial measures, followed by the metric equivalent. Follow one set or the other, but not a mixture of both because conversions may not be exact. Standard spoon and cup measurements are level and are based on the following:

1 tsp. = 5 ml, 1 tbsp. = 15 ml, 1 cup = 250 ml / 8 fl oz.

Note that Australian standard tablespoons are 20 ml, so Australian readers should use 3 tsp. in place of 1 tbsp. when measuring small quantities.

The electric oven temperatures in this book are given for conventional ovens with top and bottom heat. When using a fan oven, the temperature should be decreased by about 20–40°F / 10–20°C – check the oven manufacturer's instruction book for further guidance. The cooking times given should be used as an approximate guideline only.

Although the recipes in this book are believed to be accurate and true at the time of going to press, neither the authors nor the publisher can accept any legal responsibility or liability for any errors or omissions that may be made nor for any inaccuracies nor for any harm or injury that may come about from following instructions or advice given in this book.

CONTENTS

AUSTRIAN SACHERTORTE

Ingredients

For a 10-inch / 26-cm springform pan

Oil, to grease the pan

4 eggs

1¼ cup / 250 g sugar

¾–1 cup / 200 ml neutral taste oil, such as sunflower

¾–1 cup / 200 ml orange juice

3 cups / 300 g all-purpose (plain) flour

4 tbsp. dark cocoa powder

3 tsp. baking powder

1 cup / 300 g apricot conserve

10 oz / 300 g bittersweet (plain) cooking chocolate (70% cocoa solids)

2 tbsp. whipping cream

12 physalis

Method

Preparation time: 30 min

1 Preheat the oven to 400ºF (200ºC / gas mark 6). Oil the springform pan. Beat the eggs with the sugar for about 5 minutes until creamy, then stir in the oil, juice, flour, cocoa powder and baking powder and turn the batter into the pan.

2 Bake in the oven for about 40–45 minutes, until an inserted toothpick comes out clean.

3 Remove from the oven and let cool on a cooling rack.

4 Split the cake horizontally into two layers. Spread half of the apricot conserve on the bottom layer, replace the top layer and thinly cover the sides of the torte with apricot conserve as well.

5 Chop the chocolate. Melt in a bowl over a pan of hot water and stir in the cream.

6 Let cool slightly then coat the torte with the chocolate cream. Let set and serve decorated with physalis.

CHOCOLATE FONDUE WITH FRUIT

Ingredients

1lb 12 oz / 800 g mixed fresh fruit, such as pear, nectarine, gooseberry, banana and fig

¾–1 cup / 200 ml whipping cream

8 oz / 250 g bittersweet (plain) cooking chocolate (70% cocoa solids)

½ tsp. orange zest, finely grated

4 tbsp. orange juice

4 tsp. orange liqueur, according to taste

4 tbsp. coconut flakes

4 tbsp. nuts, chopped

Method

Prep and cook time: 30 min

1 Wash and trim the fruit, peel if necessary, and cut into bite-size pieces.

2 Arrange the fruit decoratively on a plate.

3 Put the cream and the broken chocolate pieces into a saucepan and melt the chocolate over a low heat, stirring continually. Stir in the orange zest and the orange juice.

4 Transfer the chocolate to a fondue pot and place over a burner. Add a little orange liqueur to taste.

5 Slide pieces of fruit onto a fondue fork or wooden toothpick and dip into the sauce. Serve with chopped nuts and coconut flakes.

CHOCOLATE - BANANA CAKE

Ingredients
For a loaf pan 10 x 5½ inches / 25 x 14 cm

Oil, to grease the loaf pan

2½ cups / 250 g all-purpose (plain) flour

1 cup / 250 ml milk

½ cup / 100 g sugar

⅓ cup / 80 ml oil

2 tbsp. soy flour

4 tbsp. water

3 tsp. baking powder

3–4 tbsp. dark cocoa powder

2 bananas

Method
Prep and cook time: 60 min

1 Preheat the oven to 350°F (180°C / gas mark 4). Oil and chill a loaf pan.

2 Put all the dry ingredients into a bowl. In a separate bowl mix all the wet ingredients, then quickly mix with the dry ingredients. Peel the bananas, halve lengthways and cut into pieces.

3 Fold the banana pieces into the cake batter.

4 Spread the batter evenly in the loaf pan and bake for 30–40 minutes, until an inserted toothpick comes out clean.

5 Let cool slightly, then turn out onto a platter and cool completely. Slice and serve with coffee.

CHOCOLATE MOUSSE CAKE

Ingredients

For loaf pan 8 inch 20 cm in length

6 tbsp. rum, for soaking

1/3 cup / 50 g raisins

10 oz / 300 g bittersweet (plain) cooking chocolate (70% cocoa solids)

1 small cup / 250 ml strong espresso

2 tsp. rum

5 eggs

3 tbsp. vanilla sugar

1/2 cup / 125 ml chilled whipping cream

1/4 cup / 50 g sugar

2 cups / 250 g raspberries

Method

Prep and cook time: 40 min plus 4 h 45 min refrigeration

1 Soak the raisins in the rum. Roughly chop the cooking chocolate and melt in a bowl over a pan of hot water along with the rum and espresso. Remove from the heat.

2 Separate the eggs and beat the egg yolks with the vanilla sugar until pale and creamy and the sugar has dissolved.

3 Whip the chilled cream until stiff. Beat the egg whites with the sugar until stiff.

4 Stir the egg yolk mixture into the chocolate with a whisk. Put the whipped cream on top of the chocolate mixture and whisk in quickly, before the mixture sets. Drain the raisins well and fold in.

5 Carefully fold in the beaten egg white. Line the loaf pan with plastic wrap, turn the chocolate mixture into it and cover closely with plastic wrap.

6 Put into the refrigerator for at least 4 hours, then transfer to the freezer for 45 minutes before serving.

7 Wash the raspberries. Turn the chocolate mousse cake out on to a platter and carefully remove the plastic wrap. Decorate with raspberries, slice and serve immediately.

RASPBERRY CREAM WITH WHITE CHOCOLATE

Ingredients

7 oz / 200 g white chocolate

Scant 1 cup / 200 g plain yogurt

4 tbsp. honey

2 cups / 250 g raspberries

Scant 1 cup / 200 g quark
(curd) cheese

3 tbsp. raspberry liqueur

Scant 1 cup / 200 ml whipping cream

Method

Prep and cook time: 25 min plus 2 hours chilling

1 Grate the chocolate. Reserve 2 tablespoons for decoration and put the rest into a bowl and melt, standing over a saucepan of hot water. Add the yogurt and honey and warm briefly.

2 Reserve 4 tablespoons raspberries and push the rest through a sieve to form a purée. Stir into the quark with the chocolate mixture and the raspberry liqueur.

3 Whisk the cream until stiff and fold into the mixture. Immediately spoon into individual molds and chill in the refrigerator for at least 2 hours.

4 Serve decorated with the reserved raspberries and reserved grated chocolate.

WHITE CHOCOLATE MUFFINS

Ingredients

For a 12-hole mini muffin pan

1 cup / 200 g sugar

1/3–1/2 cup / 100 ml whipping cream

1½ tbsp. / 20 g butter

Seeds from a vanilla bean (pod)

1¾ cups / 200 g self-rising flour

2 tsp. baking powder

2 tbsp. cornstarch (cornflour)

1 small ripe banana

Pinch of salt

3 eggs

To decorate:

7 oz / 200 g white coverture chocolate (30–40% cocoa butter)

1 tsp. Bourbon vanilla

1–2 tbsp. whipping cream

White chocolate shavings

Method

Prep and cook time: 60 min

1 Preheat the oven to 350°F (180°C / gas mark 4). Place a paper baking cup in each hole of the muffin pan.

2 Put 2/3 cup (125 g) of the sugar, the cream and butter into a pan and bring to a boil. Add the seeds from the vanilla bean and simmer over a low heat for 5 minutes. Cool to lukewarm.

3 Mix the flour, baking powder and cornstarch. Peel and purée the banana and whisk into the vanilla cream with the rest of the sugar and the salt. Stir in the eggs. Quickly stir in the flour mixture.

4 Put the mixture into the paper cases in the pan. Bake in the oven for 30 minutes, and then take out of the oven. Let cool in the muffin pan for 5 minutes, and then take the muffins out and cool on a cake rack.

5 Melt the white couverture chocolate in a bowl over a pan of hot water. Mix smoothly with the cream and vanilla and trickle tablespoonfuls over the muffins. Decorate with chocolate shavings and cool completely before serving.

CHOCOLATE LAYER CAKE

Ingredients

For a loaf pan 8 x 4 inches
/ 20 x 10 cm

1¼ cup / 120 g all-purpose
(plain) flour

1/3 cup / 80 g cold butter, chopped

2 tbsp. cocoa powder

3 tbsp. sugar

Pinch of salt

1 egg yolk

1/3 cup / 100 g apricot conserve

10 oz / 300 g white cooking chocolate

½ cup / 125 ml whipping cream

Seeds from a vanilla bean (pod)

4 tsp. rum

2/3 cup / 150 g butter

Method

Prep and cook time: 1 h 15 min plus 12 h refrigeration

1 Combine the flour, chopped butter, cocoa powder, sugar, salt and egg yolk and work to a pliable dough. Form into a ball, wrap in plastic wrap and put into the refrigerator for 30 minutes.

2 Roll the dough out on a floured work surface to a thickness of 1/8 inch (3 mm). Cut out 5 rectangles measuring 5 x 2½ inches (12 x 6 cm).

3 Preheat the oven to 350°F (180°C / gas mark 4). Put the rectangles on a cookie sheet lined with baking parchment and bake on the middle shelf of the oven for about 15 minutes.

4 Take out and cool on a cake rack, then spread each rectangle with the apricot conserve.

5 Melt the white chocolate in a bowl over a pan of hot water. Put the cream into a pan with the vanilla seeds and bring to a boil. Mix with the melted chocolate and rum and let cool.

6 Cream the butter and mix with the cooled chocolate cream. Chill for 30 minutes. Line the loaf pan with plastic wrap and fill with alternate layers of white chocolate cream and baked chocolate rectangles. Cover and chill overnight.

BROWNIES WITH CHERRIES

Ingredients

For a rectangular baking pan
13 x 9 inches / 34 x 24 cm

For the brownies:

Butter, to grease the baking pan

7 oz / 200 g bittersweet (plain)
cooking chocolate (70% cocoa solids)

Scant 1 cup / 200 g butter

4 eggs

1 cup / 200 g sugar

1 cup / 100 g all-purpose (plain) flour

For the cherry sauce:

1 jar Morello cherries

1 tsp. sugar

1 tbsp. potato starch flour

Good pinch of cinnamon

Method

Prep and cook time: 50 min

1 Preheat the oven to 410°F (210°C / gas mark 6).
Grease the baking pan with a little butter.

2 Melt the chocolate in a bowl over a pan of hot
water, then remove from the heat and stir in the cold
butter, a few pieces at a time. Mix until creamy.

3 Separate the eggs. Beat the egg whites until stiff.
Beat the egg yolks with the sugar until pale, thick and
creamy. Carefully stir the egg yolks into the cooled
chocolate and butter mixture. Fold in the egg whites.
Sieve the flour over the mixture and carefully fold in.

4 Turn the mixture into the pan and bake on the
middle shelf of the oven for 20 minutes. Leave to cool
in the pan.

5 For the cherry sauce, put the cherries into a
saucepan with their juice (keeping back
3 tablespoons), add the sugar and heat. Put the
cinnamon, potato starch flour and the 3 tablespoons
juice into a cup, mix smoothly and then stir into the
cherries. Bring to a boil once and set aside.

6 Cut the cake into 15 squares and then into
triangles. Serve garnished with the cherry sauce.

CHOCOLATE-GLAZED PEARS

Ingredients

4 large, firm pears suitable for cooking

Juice of 1 lemon

3½ oz / 100 g bittersweet (plain) couverture chocolate (30–40% cocoa butter)

3½ oz / 100 g white couverture chocolate (30–40% cocoa butter)

Bay leaves

For the sauce:

3½ oz / 100 g candied peel

3½ tbsp. dry white wine

2 tbsp. butter

Method

Prep and cook time: 30 min

1 Wash and peel the pears, but leave the stalks on. Level off the bottoms and drizzle lemon juice over the top.

2 Place on a cookie sheet and bake in the oven at 375°F (180°C / gas mark 5) for about 15 minutes.

3 Remove from the oven.

4 Melt the two types of chocolate in separate bowls over a pan of boiling water. Coat two pears with the dark chocolate and two pears with the white chocolate. Attach the bay leaves to the stalks and let dry.

5 Boil the wine together with the chopped candied peel until the liquid has a syrup consistency. Season to taste with butter. Arrange the pears on a plate, drizzle a little of the syrup around the pears and serve.

CARAMELIZED CHOCOLATE CREAM

Ingredients
For 4–6 ramekins 5–6 oz / 150–180 ml

1 cup / 250 ml milk

1 cup / 250 ml whipping cream

1 vanilla bean (pod)

3 tbsp. dark cocoa powder

1/3 cup / 75 g sugar

3 eggs

2 egg yolks

1 tbsp. cornstarch (cornflour)

Cane sugar, to sprinkle

Method
Prep and cook time: 1 h 10 min

1 Preheat the oven to 400°F (200°C / gas mark 6). Put the milk, cream, the scraped pulp from the vanilla bean, cocoa powder and the vanilla bean into a pan and bring to the boil.

2 Beat the eggs and the egg yolks until creamy but not frothy, stir in the cornstarch and gradually stir into the hot vanilla-flavoured milk. Pour through a sieve into the ramekins.

3 Put the ramekins in a baking dish and add enough hot water to come 2/3 of the way up the sides. Bake in the oven for about 30 minutes, until set. Take out of the oven, let cool and then put in the refrigerator.

4 Before serving, sprinkle brown sugar over the cream and briefly put under the hot broiler (grill), until the top is caramelized. Alternatively, stand the ramekins in an oven pan of ice-cold water and briefly put in a very hot oven until the sugar forms a crust.

WHITE CHOCOLATE CREAM WITH CHOCOLATE SAUCE AND CHERRIES

Ingredients

For 4 molds around 1 cup /225 ml size

For the vanilla cream:

2/3 cup / 150 ml milk

1 vanilla bean (pod)

1/3 cup / 60 g sugar

3½ oz / 100 g white cooking chocolate

6 sheets gelatin

¾–1 cup / 200 ml whipping cream

¾–1 cup / 200 g natural yogurt

For the chocolate sauce:

5 oz / 150 g bittersweet (plain) cooking chocolate (70% cocoa solids)

½ cup / 125 ml milk

1/3–½ cup / 100 g whipping cream

½ vanilla bean (pod)

1/3 cup / 75 g softened butter

A few cherries, to garnish

Method

Prep and cook time: 45 min plus 4 h refrigeration

1 For the vanilla cream, heat the milk in a pan with the seeds scraped out of the vanilla bean, the vanilla bean and the sugar. Then remove from the heat, break up the chocolate and melt in the hot milk. Let cool.

2 Soak the gelatin in cold water. Whip the cream, but not too stiffly.

3 Squeeze out the gelatin and put into a small pan with about 3 tablespoons of the chocolate milk. Heat gently over a low heat until the gelatin has dissolved. Stir in the rest of the chocolate milk and the yoghurt and fold in the cream. Fill individual molds, cover and chill for 4 hours.

4 For the chocolate sauce, chop the chocolate. Put the milk and cream into a pan with the vanilla bean (slit open) and bring to a boil. Pour the hot milk onto the cooking chocolate and melt carefully. Beat the softened butter and gradually stir the chocolate milk mixture into the butter.

5 To serve, briefly dip the molds in hot water and turn out on to dessert plates. Add chocolate sauce, garnish with cherries and serve.

CHOCOLATE CHEESECAKE

Ingredients

For an 11-inch/28-cm springform pan

For the base:

7 oz / 200 g ladyfingers (boudoir biscuits)

3½ oz / 100 g milk chocolate (30% cocoa solids)

⅓– ½ cup / 80–125 g butter

2–3 tbsp. cocoa powder, to taste

For the cheesecake filling:

7 oz / 200 g milk chocolate (30% cocoa solids)

10 sheets gelatin

2 cups / 500 g low-fat quark, or unsalted cream cheese

¼–½ cup / 50–100 g sugar, according to taste

¾–1 cup / 200 g heavy sour cream

Cocoa powder, if needed

1⅓ cups / 300 ml whipping cream

Cocoa, for dusting

8 strawberries, to garnish

Method

Prep and cook time: 50 min plus 4 h 30 min refrigeration

1 For the base reduce the ladyfingers to crumbs in a food processor. Melt the chocolate in a bowl over a pan of hot water, stir in the butter and then the ladyfinger crumbs. Add a little cocoa powder if necessary.

2 Put a cake ring on a cake plate and press the crumb mixture firmly and evenly onto the base and sides (it should be 1½–2 inches (4–5 cm) high, making sure it is thick enough at the edge. Chill for at least 30 minutes.

3 For the cheesecake filling, melt the chocolate in a bowl over a pan of hot water. Soak the gelatin in plenty of cold water. Mix the quark smoothly with the sugar. Squeeze out the gelatin, put into a small pan and heat over a medium heat until dissolved. Stir into the melted chocolate. Stir in the sour cream and then quickly stir the chocolate mixture into the quark. Stir in a little cocoa powder to make the filling more chocolate-tasting if desired. As soon as the mixture begins to set, whip the cream until stiff and fold in.

4 Spread the mixture evenly on the prepared base and chill for at least 4 hours. To serve, dust the cheesecake thickly with cocoa. Wash, dry and halve the strawberries and arrange on top of the cake. Carefully remove the cake ring, cut the cake into pieces and serve.

CHOCOLATE PEAR CAKE

Ingredients

For 9 inch / 24 cm springform pan

For the base:

¼ cup / 60 g butter

1¼ cups / 140 g all-purpose (plain) flour

¼ cup / 50 g sugar

2 egg yolks

For the filling:

3 ripe pears

1 egg

⅓ cup / 75 g butter

⅓ cup / 75 g brown cane sugar

¼ cup / 20 g ground almonds

⅔ cup / 75 g flour

½ tsp. baking powder

¼ cup / 25 g dark cocoa powder

¼ cup / 50 ml milk

Confectioners' (icing) sugar, to dust

Method

Prep and cook time: 1 h 30 min

1 For the base, quickly combine all the base ingredients and work to a dough. Wrap in plastic wrap and put into the refrigerator for 30 minutes.

2 Preheat the oven to 375°F (190°C / gas mark 5). Grease or line the springform pan. Roll out the dough to a circle on a lightly floured work surface and use to line the base of the pan.

3 For the filling, peel the pears, halve lengthways and remove the cores.

4 Cream the butter and sugar, beat in the egg and stir in the flour, ground almonds, baking powder, cocoa powder and milk. Spread on top of the dough in the springform pan, arrange the pear halves on top and press in. Bake on the middle shelf of the oven for about 45 minutes. Cover with aluminum foil after 30 minutes to prevent the top burning.

5 When done take out of the oven, let cool slightly, then take the cake out of the springform pan and cool completely. Dust with confectioners' sugar before serving.

MELTING CHOCOLATE PUDDING

Ingredients

For six ramekins

Butter to brush the ramekins, melted

4½ oz / 125 g bittersweet (plain) cooking chocolate, (70% cocoa solids)

Generous ½ cup / 125 g butter

2 eggs

3 egg yolks

⅓ cup / 65 g sugar

Pinch of salt

¼ cup / 25 g all-purpose (plain) flour

Cocoa powder, for dusting

Whipping cream, to serve

Method

Prep and cook time: 55 min plus 12 h refrigeration

1 Brush 6 porcelain ramekins with melted butter and chill.

2 Chop the chocolate very finely and melt in a bowl over a pan of hot water with the butter. Beat the eggs, egg yolks, sugar and a pinch of salt for 8–10 minutes, until thick and creamy.

3 Then gradually fold in the melted chocolate and butter. Sieve the flour onto the mixture and fold in. Turn the mixture into the prepared ramekins and chill overnight.

4 Next day preheat the oven to 350°F (180°C / gas mark 4) and bake the puddings for about 15 minutes, until the middle puffs up slightly (do not open the oven while the puddings are baking).

5 The outer layer should be baked, but the center should be still liquid. Take the ramekins out of the oven and carefully turn out the pudding. Put on plates, dust with cocoa and serve with whipped cream.

CHOCOLATE FRAPPÉ WITH WHIPPED CREAM

Ingredients

For four tall glasses

1/3–1/2 cup / 100 ml whipping cream

1 tsp. vanilla extract

2 cups / 500 ml milk

2–3 large glasses of crushed ice

Chocolate syrup, according to taste

Cinnamon, to decorate

Method

Prep and cook time: 15 min

1 Whip the cream with the vanilla extract until stiff and put in a pastry bag with a rosette tube.

2 Pour the milk in a blender and add the crushed ice (divide into 2–3 batches). Add chocolate syrup according to taste and blend well until smooth.

3 Pour into 4 glasses. The layers will form as the frappé stands. Pipe the whipped cream over the top, sprinkle with cinnamon and serve.

CHOCOLATE SOUFFLÉ

Ingredients

For four ramekins

3 fresh egg yolks

½ cup / 100 g sugar

2¼ oz / 60 g bittersweet (plain) cooking chocolate (70% cocoa solids)

¾–1 cup / 200 ml whipping cream

Cocoa, for dusting

3 tsp. honey, for garnish

4 orange segments, for garnish

Chocolate curls, for garnish

Chocolate sticks, for garnish

Method

Prep and cook time: 40 min plus 5 h to freeze

1 Wrap the ramekins in aluminium foil, extending the foil above the rim of the dish.

2 Beat the egg yolks with the sugar for about 10 minutes until pale and creamy. Melt the chocolate in a bowl over a pan of hot water, let cool slightly then carefully fold into the egg yolk mixture.

3 Whip the cream until stiff and fold into the egg mixture. Divide the mixture between the 4 prepared ramekins. Put into the freezer for 4–5 hours.

4 Take the ramekins out of the freezer and let stand at room temperature for 3–4 minutes. Remove the foil. Dust with cocoa and serve garnished with an orange segment, a little honey, a chocolate stick and a chocolate curl.

CHOCOLATE ICE CREAM SOUFFLÉ

Ingredients

For four glasses or dishes

1/3 cup / 65 g sugar

2 tbsp. water

3 egg yolks

2 tbsp. sugar

2 oz / 50 g white cooking chocolate

2 oz / 50 g milk chocolate (30% cocoa solids)

3 tbsp. rum

1¼ cups / 275 ml whipping cream

Cocoa powder, to sprinkle

Cinnamon, to sprinkle

Pepper, to sprinkle (optional)

Method

Prep and cook time: 40 min plus 5 h refrigeration

1 Dissolve 1/3 cup (65 g) sugar in 2 tablespoons of water and bring to the boil. Whisk the egg yolks together with 2 tablespoons of sugar until frothy, and then slowly drizzle into the sugar solution. Continue to whisk until the mixture has cooled.

2 Break the chocolate into small pieces and melt in a bowl over a pan of hot water. Fold into the egg mixture, together with the rum. Whip the cream and fold into the mixture.

3 Wrap 4 glasses or dishes with aluminium foil, which has been folded over 2 or 3 times at the top (in order to make it stronger). Make sure the foil extends about 1 inch (2–3 cm) above the edge of each glass.

4 Pour the mixture into the glasses and freeze for about 5 hours.

5 Remove the aluminium foil and sprinkle pepper, cocoa powder and cinnamon over the top before serving.

MINI CHOCOLATE MUFFINS

Ingredients

For a 24-hole mini muffin pan

3½ oz / 100 g bittersweet (plain) cooking chocolate (70% cocoa solids), grated

3½ oz / 100 g margarine

1/3 cup / 65 g sugar

1 tsp. vanilla extract

Pinch of salt

1 egg

2 cups / 200 g all-purpose (plain) flour

1 level tsp. baking powder

½ tsp. baking soda

1 level tbsp. dark cocoa

1/3–½ cup / 100 ml cup milk

1/3 cup / 50 g chopped peanuts, or peanut halves

Method

Prep and cook time: 50 min

1 Line the muffin pan with paper baking cups. Preheat the oven to 350°F (180°C / gas mark 4).

2 Cream the margarine with the grated chocolate in a mixing bowl. Gradually work in the sugar, vanilla extract and salt to produce a cohesive mixture. Add the egg and mix well, if using a food processor on the highest speed.

3 Mix the flour with the baking powder, baking soda and cocoa and add to the mixture in two portions, alternating with the milk and mixing briefly at each stage. Fold in the nuts.

4 Put the mixture into a freezer bag, seal it well and cut off one corner. Then pipe the mixture evenly into the paper cases in the prepared muffin pan.

5 Bake in the oven on the middle shelf for about 25 minutes.

6 Take out of the oven and let rest for 10 minutes, then take out of the muffin pan and let cool completely on a cake rack.

CHOCOLATE CAKE WITH ORANGE CREAM

Ingredients

For 9 inches / 24 cm springform pan

For the cake batter:

8 oz / 200 g soft butter

¾ cup / 60 g finely ground almonds

7 oz / 200 g bittersweet (plain) cooking chocolate (70% cocoa solids)

1 cup / 150 g confectioners' (icing) sugar

8 eggs

½ cup / 100 g sugar

1½ cups / 150 g all-purpose (plain) flour

For the orange cream:

12 oz / 350 g mascarpone

2 large oranges, zested and chopped into small pieces

2 tsp. zest and juice of another orange

2 tsp. Grand Marnier

Sugar, to taste

For the frosting:

7 oz / 200 g bittersweet (plain) cooking chocolate (70% cocoa solids)

1 cup / 200 g sugar

⅓–½ cup / 100 ml water

For the decoration:

Candied orange peel

Silver sugar balls

Method

Prep and cook time: 2 h 30 min

1 Heat the oven to 350°F (180°C / gas mark 4). Grease the pan with a little of the butter and scatter 1/6 of the almonds over the bottom. Keep cool.

2 For the cake batter, melt the chopped chocolate in a bowl over a pan of hot water. Cream the butter with the confectioners' sugar until light and fluffy. Separate the eggs. Gradually stir the egg yolks and melted chocolate into the butter.

3 Beat the egg whites with the sugar until stiff, then carefully fold into the chocolate mixture. Mix the flour with the almonds and likewise fold in. Turn the batter into the prepared pan and bake in the oven for about 1 hour. Remove from the oven, let cool and take out of the pan.

4 Mix the mascarpone with the orange pieces and juice, Grand Marnier, orange zest and sugar.

5 Split the cake horizontally into three layers. Spread the orange cream on the bottom layer, place the middle layer on top, spread with the rest of the orange cream and replace the top layer.

6 For the frosting, grate the chocolate finely and melt in a bowl over a pan of hot water. Bring the sugar and water to a boil for about 5–8 minutes, and then stir into the chocolate a spoonful at a time until the mixture thickens. Spread the frosting on the cake immediately.

7 Make star shapes from the orange peel and decorate the cake with orange stars and silver sugar balls.

CHOCOLATES WITH CANDIED FRUIT FILLING

Ingredients

For a dish or cake pan 6 x 6 inches / 15 x 15 cm square

12 oz / 350 g gianduja (hazelnut chocolate)

5 oz / 150 g bittersweet (plain) cooking chocolate (70% cocoa solids)

1 tbsp. hot espresso

1/3 cup / 50 g pine nuts

1 cup / 150 g lightly candied fruit, such as melon, apricots

For the topping:

7 oz / 200 g bittersweet (plain) cooking chocolate (70% cocoa solids)

Method

Prep and cook time: 1 h plus at least 3 h cooling

1 Chop the chocolate and put into a metal bowl with the gianduja. Add the espresso and melt in a bowl over a pan of hot water, stirring slowly but frequently.

2 Toast the pine nuts in a skillet over a medium heat, stirring, until golden brown. Chop the candied fruit.

3 Line the square dish or cake pan with plastic wrap or aluminium foil.

4 Fold the pine nuts and candied fruit into the chocolate mixture and spread smoothly in the dish. Put in a cool place (not the refrigerator) for about 2 hours, to set completely.

5 For the topping, finely chop the chocolate and melt in a bowl over a pan of hot water.

6 Take the gianduja mixture out of the dish and pull off the foil. Cut into 1-inch (3-cm) cubes. Put the squares on a fork, one at a time, and dip in the melted chocolate topping. Put on wax paper for at least 1 hour to dry.

7 Put the chocolates into a dish separated with plastic wrap and store in the refrigerator.

WHITE CHOCOLATE CHEESECAKE

Ingredients

For four 3-inch / 8-cm cake rings

For the base:

1½ cups / 150 g all-purpose (plain) flour

Scant ½ cup / 100 g butter

¼ cup / 50 g sugar

1 egg yolk

For the filling:

7 oz / 200 g white cooking chocolate

1½ cups / 350 g low-fat quark or unsalted cream cheese

2 eggs

2 tbsp. cornstarch (cornflour)

1 tsp. Bourbon vanilla extract

For the topping:

2½ cups / 300 g raspberries (frozen work well)

2 tbsp. cornstarch (cornflour)

3 tbsp. sugar

1 handful fresh raspberries, to decorate

2 tbsp. confectioners' (icing) sugar, to decorate

Method

Prep and cook time: 1 h plus 2 h refrigeration

1 Preheat the oven to 325°F (160°C / gas mark 3). Put all the ingredients for the base into a bowl, chop with a knife and then knead to a smooth dough. Divide into 4 portions, roll each portion into a ball and roll out to roughly 3-inch (8-cm) circles.

2 Place on a cookie sheet lined with baking parchment and put a 3-inch (8-cm) stainless steel cake ring around each circle. Press the pastry in firmly at the edge.

3 For the filling, melt the chocolate in a bowl over a pan of hot water. Quickly mix the rest of the filling ingredients with a whisk or a wooden spoon, and then stir in the melted chocolate. Spread the filling smoothly on the 4 bases and bake the cheesecakes in the oven for 30–40 minutes. Cover with aluminium foil to prevent the top browning too much, if necessary.

4 When done let the cakes stand briefly in the oven. Then chill for at least 2 hours in the refrigerator, until completely cold.

5 Meanwhile make the raspberry glaze. Finely purée the raspberries and push through a sieve. Mix smoothly with the sugar and cornstarch, put into a pan and briefly bring to a boil, stirring constantly. Set aside and let cool slightly.

6 Then put each cake, still in its cake ring, on a plate, spread the raspberry glaze on the surface and carefully loosen and remove the cake ring. Decorate the surface with fresh raspberries and serve dusted with confectioners' (icing) sugar.

PANCAKES WITH CHOCOLATE CREAM AND ORANGE ZEST

Ingredients

For approximately 8–12 pancakes

For the pancake batter:

1¼ cups / 120 g all-purpose (plain) flour

1 tbsp. sugar

Pinch of salt

1 tbsp. orange liqueur

3 eggs

1 egg yolk

2 tbsp. melted butter

½ cup / 125 ml milk

⅓ cup / 80 ml sparkling mineral water

For the filling:

3½ oz / 100 g bittersweet (plain) cooking chocolate (70% cocoa solids)

2 tbsp. strong espresso

2 tbsp. chocolate liqueur

2 eggs

1 tsp. vanilla extract

⅓ cup / 80 ml chilled whipping cream

2–3 tbsp. heavy sour cream

1 tbsp. sugar

Confectioners' (icing) sugar, for dusting

Orange zest, to garnish

Method

Prep and cook time: 1 h plus 1 h to stand

1 For the pancake batter, mix the flour, sugar, orange liqueur, salt, eggs, egg yolk and butter. Gradually stir in the milk with a whisk. Let the batter rest for 1 hour.

2 Heat a large skillet and put a little butter into it. While it is melting stir the sparkling water into the batter. Pour a small ladleful of batter into the skillet and tilt it this way and that so that the batter covers the base of the skillet. When bubbles form, turn the pancake over and cook the other side. Take out and cool. Repeat the process until all the batter is used up.

3 For the filling, roughly chop the chocolate and melt in a bowl over a pan of hot water with the espresso. Remove from the heat, stir in the liqueur and let cool.

4 Separate the eggs. Beat the egg yolks with the vanilla extract over a pan of hot water until thick and foamy. Whip the chilled cream until stiff. Beat the egg whites with the sugar until they form stiff peaks. Add the egg yolks to the chocolate and stir in with a whisk

5 Put the whipped cream and sour cream on top of the chocolate mixture and quickly mix in with the whisk, before the mixture sets. Carefully fold in the beaten egg whites.

6 To serve, spread a little of the chocolate cream on each pancake, fold over and put on plates. Dust with confectioners' sugar and garnish with orange zest.

CHOCOLATE-PECAN TART

Ingredients

For an 12-inch / 30-cm tart pan

For the pastry:

1¾ cups / 180 g all-purpose (plain) flour

2 tbsp. cocoa powder

1/3 cup / 70 g superfine (castor) sugar

Pinch of salt

1 egg

4 oz / 120 g butter

Flour for the work surface

Butter, to grease the tart pan

Dried pulses for baking blind

For the filling:

2½–3 oz / 70 g bittersweet (plain) cooking chocolate (70% cocoa solids)

Scant ½ cup / 100 g butter

½ cup / 100 g sugar

A pinch of salt

4 eggs

½ cup / 60 g self-rising flour

1/3–½ cup / 50 g roughly chopped pecans

1²/3 cups / 200 g pecan halves, to garnish

Method

Prep and cook time: 1 h 20 min

1 Mix the flour with the cocoa, salt and sugar and make a well in the center. Break the egg into the well, add the butter in small pieces and quickly work to a dough. Wrap in foil or plastic wrap and let rest in the refrigerator for 30 minutes.

2 Preheat the oven to 350ºF (180°C / gas mark 4). Roll out the pastry on a lightly floured work surface and use to line the base and sides of a greased tart pan. Lay a piece of baking parchment on the pastry and fill the pastry shell with dried pulses. Bake in the oven for about 20 minutes.

3 Meanwhile for the filling, melt the chocolate in a bowl over a pan of hot water and let cool. Cream the butter with the sugar and salt until light and fluffy, then beat in the eggs one after another to produce a light, fluffy mixture. Fold in the chocolate, flour and chopped pecans.

4 Take the pastry shell out of the oven, remove the dried pulses and baking parchment and turn the chocolate filling into the pastry shell, smoothing the top. Arrange the pecan halves on top of the filling and press them in lightly. Bake the tart at 300ºF (150°C / gas mark 2) for about 30 minutes, or until an inserted toothpick comes out clean.

CHOCOLATE CREAM

Ingredients
For four 9 fl oz / 250 ml glasses

7 oz / 200 g block of dark chocolate;
65–80% cocoa solids

10 oz / 300 g hazelnut nougat

1½ cups / 350 ml evaporated milk

7 oz / 200 g butter

Method
Prep and cook time: 30 min

1 Melt the chocolate and the nougat slowly in a pot together with the butter, stirring every now and then. When all the ingredients have melted and blended, remove from the heat and let cool.

2 Stir in the evaporated milk. Pour the mixture into glasses and cover well. Keep in the refrigerator.

CHOCOLATE TRUFFLES

Ingredients

For a baking frame 8 x 8 inches
/ 20 x 20 cm square

7 oz / 200 g milk chocolate
(30% cocoa solids)

8 oz / 250 g bittersweet (plain)
cooking chocolate (70% cocoa solids)

¾–1 cup / 200 ml whipping cream

½ tsp. star anise

3 bags black tea

Dark cocoa powder, for dusting

Method

Prep and cook time: 45 min plus 24 h to stand

1 Chop both types of chocolate very finely and put into a bowl. Put the cream into a small pan and bring to a boil. Then remove from the heat at once and hang the tea bags in the cream. Infuse for about 5 minutes, then squeeze out well and take out again.

2 Reheat the tea-flavored cream and add the chocolate and star anise. Stir until the chocolate melts, and then let the mixture cool slightly.

3 Line the baking frame with waxed paper and put on a marble slab. Pour the mixture into the frame, cover with plastic wrap and let set for about 24 hours.

4 Cut into 50–60 even cubes. Dust with cocoa powder and serve. Keep in the refrigerator.

DOUGHNUT PROFITEROLE

Ingredients

For eight doughnuts

¾ oz / 20 g yeast

⅓–½ cup / 100 ml lukewarm milk

2–3 tbsp. sugar

2¼ cups / 220 g all-purpose (plain) flour

3 egg yolks

1¾ tbsp. soft butter

Pinch of salt

½ tsp. grated lemon zest

4 cups oil / 1 liter for deep-frying

For the filling:

1 cup / 250 ml milk

2–3 tbsp. sugar

2 tbsp. cornstarch (cornflour)

¼ tsp. vanilla extract

1 egg yolk

For the topping:

2 oz / 60 g bittersweet (plain) cooking chocolate (70% cocoa solids)

2 tbsp. butter

Fresh raspberries, to garnish

Mint leaves, to garnish

Confectioners' (icing) sugar, for dusting

Method

Prep and cook time: 2 h

1 Dissolve the yeast in the milk with the sugar. Then combine with the flour, egg yolks, butter, salt and lemon zest and knead to a soft dough using the dough hook of your food mixer. Continue kneading until the dough comes away from the sides of the bowl. Cover and put to rise in a warm place until the dough has doubled in volume.

2 Then knock back (knead again) on a floured work surface, halve and shape the two halves into rolls. Cut each roll into 4 equal pieces, roll into balls and let rise for about 30 minutes.

3 Heat the oil to 350°F (180°C) and put the dough balls into the hot fat upside down (you will need to do this in batches). As soon as one side is golden brown, turn over and fry the other side. Take out of the frying fat with a slotted spoon or skimmer and drain on paper towel. Leave to cool.

4 For the filling, take 3–4 tablespoons of the milk and mix smoothly with the sugar and cornstarch. Bring the rest of the milk to a boil, add the vanilla extract and the mixed cornstarch and briefly return to a boil. Remove from the heat and thicken with the egg yolk. Let cool, stirring occasionally.

5 Split the doughnuts, fill with the cooled cream mixture and put the lids on. Chop the chocolate and melt in a bowl over a pan of hot water with the butter. Pour over the profiteroles and serve decorated with raspberries, mint leaves and confectioners' (icing) sugar.

HAZELNUT-CHOCOLATE CAKE

Ingredients

For a 10-inch / 26-cm springform pan

¾ cup / 70 g ground hazelnuts

6 oz / 175 g bittersweet (plain) cooking chocolate (70% cocoa solids)

¾ cup / 175 g butter

4 large eggs

¾ cup / 150 g sugar

1 tsp. vanilla extract

⅓ cup / 40 g self-rising flour

¼ tsp. salt

1 tsp. baking powder

For the chocolate topping:

⅔ cup / 140 ml whipping cream

8 oz / 250 g bittersweet (plain) cooking chocolate (70% cocoa solids)

2 tbsp. butter

1 tbsp. cognac

For the nut topping:

¼ cup / 50 g sugar

2 tbsp. butter

¼ cup / 100 g whole hazelnuts

Method

Prep and cook time: 1 h 40 min plus 2 h to cool

1 Lightly toast the hazelnuts in a dry skillet until they begin to release their aroma. Then set aside and let cool.

2 Chop the chocolate and melt slowly in a bowl over a pan of hot water. Remove from the heat and stir in the cold butter in small pieces.

3 Separate the eggs. Beat the egg yolks with the sugar and vanilla extract, using an electric mixer at the highest speed, for about 7 minutes until very creamy. Beat the egg whites until stiff. Mix the flour with the nuts, salt and baking powder. Fold the chocolate into the egg yolk mixture, then add the flour mixture and beaten egg whites on top of the chocolate mixture and carefully fold in.

4 Preheat the oven to 400°F (200°C / gas mark 6). Line the springform pan with baking parchment. Turn the batter into the pan and bake at for 30–40 minutes, until an inserted toothpick comes out clean. Take out of the oven and let cool in the pan.

5 For the chocolate topping, put the cream into a pan and bring to a boil. Boil for 2–3 minutes, then add the chopped chocolate and stir until melted. Stir in the butter and cognac and let cool. Whip the mixture lightly. Release the cake from the springform pan and turn out onto a platter. Coat with the chocolate topping.

6 For the nut topping, put the sugar into a pan and melt, stirring. Add the butter and caramelize to a light brown color. Add the nuts, mix briefly, and then scatter on top of the cake. Let cool completely, cut into pieces and serve.

MOUSSE AU CHOCOLAT WITH PASSION FRUIT

Ingredients

For 4 small glasses

1–2 tsp. cornstarch (cornflour)

¾ cup / 200 ml milk

1 egg, separated

2 oz / 50 g milk chocolate (30% cocoa solids), chopped

2 oz / 50 g bittersweet (plain) cooking chocolate (70% cocoa solids), chopped

¼ cup / 50 ml whipping cream

1–2 passion fruit, to garnish

Method

Prep and cook time: 30 min plus 5 h to cool

1 Mix the cornstarch with 1–2 tablespoons of cold milk and heat the rest of the milk. Stir the cornstarch into the boiling milk, bring to a boil once, mix in the egg yolk, then remove from the heat, add the finely chopped chocolate and stir until melted.

2 Whisk the egg white until stiff and fold into the cooled mixture with the stiffly whipped cream.

3 Fill the glasses and let cool for at least 5 hours.

4 Wash the passion fruit, scrape out the pulp and arrange in the top of the glasses. Serve immediately.

MARBLE CAKE

Ingredients

For 1 Bundt cake pan

Butter, to grease the cake pan

Breadcrumbs, to line the cake pan

Generous 1 cup / 250 g soft butter

1 1/3 cups / 250 g sugar

1 tsp. vanilla extract

5 eggs

5 cups / 500 g all-purpose (plain) flour

1 tsp. baking powder

2 oz / 50 g bittersweet (plain) cooking chocolate (70% cocoa solids)

1 tsp. instant coffee powder

2 tbsp. condensed milk

2 tbsp. dark cocoa powder

Method

Prep and cook time: 1 h 30 min

1 Preheat the oven to 350°F (180°C / gas mark 4). Grease the cake pan and coat with breadcrumbs.

2 Beat the butter, sugar and vanilla extract until creamy. Add the eggs, one at a time. Mix the flour with baking powder and fold in carefully.

3 Break the chocolate into pieces, mix with the coffee powder and the condensed milk and melt over a low heat. Let cool.

4 Remove one third of the cake mix and stir in the chocolate cream. Pour half of the white cake mix into the cake pan. Pour the chocolate mix on top, followed by the rest of the white cake mix. Use a fork to swirl the batter a little. Smooth the top.

5 Bake the cake in the oven for about 1 hour until well risen and firm (cover with aluminium foil if the top starts to get too brown). Cool the cake in the pan for a while, then invert onto a rack and let cool.

CHOCOLATE FUDGE CAKE

Ingredients

For a rectangular baking frame
6 x 12 inches / 15 x 30 cm

For the cake batter:

4½ oz / 125 g bittersweet (plain) cooking chocolate (70% cocoa solids)

2 tbsp. orange liqueur

4 eggs

1 pinch salt

½–¾ cup / 135 g sugar

Generous ½ cup / 125 g soft butter

2 tbsp. maple syrup

½ cup / 100 g whole hazelnuts, ground

½ cup / 35 g coconut flakes

4–6 chocolate caramels, chopped

Oil, to grease the frame

Flour, to coat the frame

For the fudge topping:

2 cups / 400 g sugar

½ cup / 50 g cocoa

1 cup / 235 ml milk

¼ cup / 60 ml soft butter

Vanilla extract, to taste

Method

Prep and cook time: 1 h 40 min

1 Chop the chocolate and melt with the liqueur in a bowl over a pan of hot water. Separate the eggs.

2 Beat the egg whites until stiff with a pinch of salt, gradually add a quarter of the sugar and continue beating until firm, glossy and white.

3 Cream the butter with the rest of the sugar until pale and creamy. Stir the egg yolks into the maple syrup and chocolate. Fold in the beaten egg whites, ground hazelnuts and coconut flakes. Preheat the oven to 325°F (160°C / gas mark 3).

4 Put the baking frame on a cookie sheet lined with baking parchment. Oil the inner sides and sprinkle with flour. Fold the chopped caramels into the batter, turn the batter into the frame and bake in the oven for about 50 minutes. After 35 minutes, cover the top with kitchen foil to prevent it browning too much. Remove from the oven and let cool.

5 For the fudge topping, put the sugar, cocoa powder and milk into a pot and bring to a boil stirring constantly. Reduce the heat, do not stir any further and check the temperature with a sugar thermometer: it must be 237°F / 114°C (alternatively, drop a little of the mixture into a cup of cold water, to see if it forms smooth, malleable lumps).

6 Remove the pot from the heat and stir in the butter and the vanilla extract. Beat with a wooden spoon until the fudge is no longer shiny. Pour onto the cake, spread evenly and let cool.

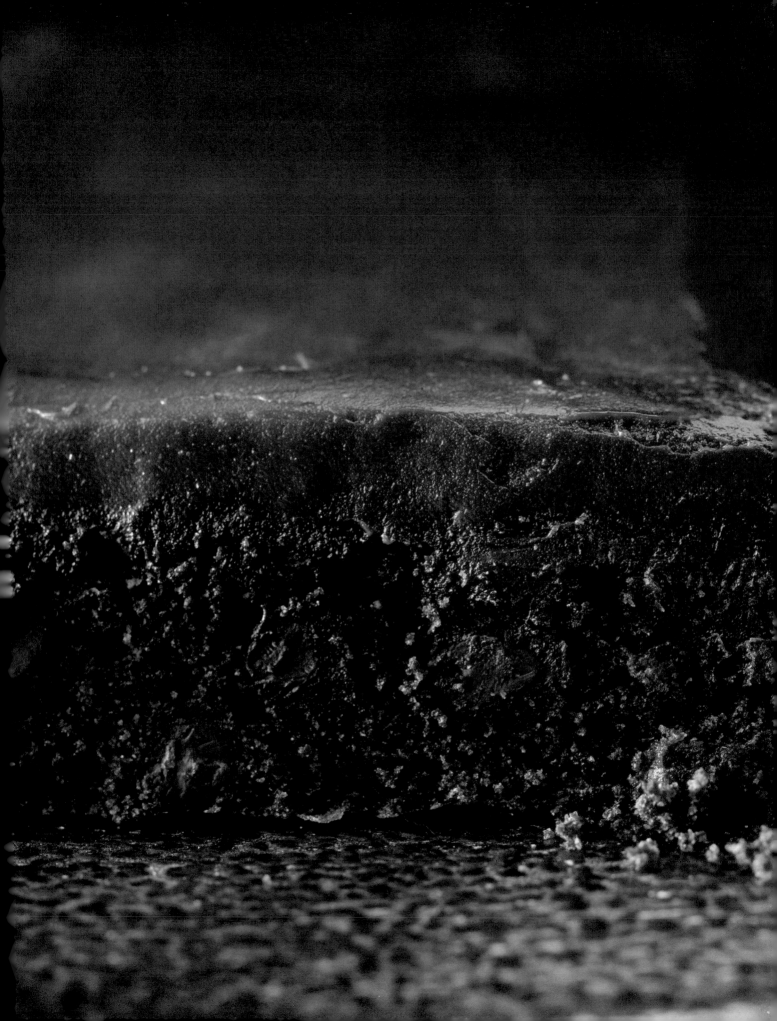

MACARONS AU CHOCOLAT

Ingredients

To make about 15 macarons

4 egg whites

2 tsp. lemon juice

1¹/₃ cup / 250 g superfine (caster) sugar

2¹/₃ cups / 200 g ground almonds

2 tsp. cocoa

For the filling:

5 oz / 150 g bittersweet (plain) cooking chocolate (70% cocoa solids)

¹/₃ cup / 80 ml whipping cream

1½ tbsp. / 20 g butter

Cocoa, for dusting

Heart stencil

Method

Prep and cook time: 1 h

1 Beat the egg whites with the lemon juice until they form stiff peaks, then gradually trickle in the sugar, still beating. Continue beating until the mixture is firm and shiny, and then carefully fold in the ground almonds. Fold in the cocoa to lightly color the mixture.

2 Preheat the oven to 270ºF (135ºC / gas mark 1½–1). Put the mixture into a piping bag with a large round nozzle and pipe 30 small domed circles approximately ¾ inch (2 cm) in diameter onto a cookie sheet lined with baking parchment.

3 Bake the macaroons in the oven for about 40 minutes, leaving the oven door open a crack.

4 For the filling, chop the chocolate into small pieces and melt carefully in a bowl over a pan of hot water. Whip the cream until stiff. Cut the butter into small pieces and stir into the melted chocolate with a whisk. As soon as the chocolate has cooled fold in the cream.

5 Sandwich the macaroons together in twos with the chocolate cream. Put the stencil on top of each macaroon, dust with cocoa, and then carefully remove the stencil.

MARBLED CHOCOLATE
WITH NUTS AND SEEDS

Ingredients

3½ oz / 100 g white cooking chocolate

3½ oz / 100 g bittersweet (plain) cooking chocolate (70% cocoa solids)

1 tbsp. palm butter

6 tbsp. mixed nuts and seeds, such as Brazil nuts, pecan nuts, sunflower seeds

1 tbsp. dried cherries

Method

Prep and cook time: 30 min plus 45 min to set

1 Chop each kind of cooking chocolate separately into small pieces. Divide the palm butter into two parts and put each half in a bowl over a pan of hot water.

2 Put 3 oz (80 g) of the chopped white chocolate in one bowl and 3 oz (80 g) of the chopped bittersweet chocolate in the other.

3 Melt the chocolate slowly over a hot but not boiling pan of water. Melt the rest of the chopped chocolate in the melted chocolate.

4 Pour the dark chocolate onto the baking paper in 8 rough circles. Pour the white chocolate on top and marble together with a wooden spoon.

5 Chop the nuts, seeds and cherries into large pieces, lightly sprinkle over the chocolate and let set.

6 Remove the cooled chocolates from the baking paper and serve with coffee.

CHOCOLATE CAKE

Ingredients

For a 10-inch / 26-cm springform pan

For the cake:

6 eggs

1 cup / 200 g sugar

1 tsp. vanilla extract

2 cups / 200 g all-purpose (plain) flour

½ tsp. baking powder

½ cup / 50 g cocoa powder

Pinch of salt

4 tbsp. cherry juice

1½ tbsp. kirsch

For the topping:

8 oz / 250 g bittersweet (plain) cooking chocolate (70% cocoa solids)

1/3–½ cup / 100 ml whipping cream

Method

Prep and cook time: 1 h 25 min

1 Preheat the oven to 350ºF (180ºC / gas mark 4). Line the springform pan with baking parchment. Beat the eggs with the sugar and vanilla extract for at least 7 minutes with an electric mixer at the highest speed, until the mixture is pale and foamy and forms peaks.

2 Mix the flour, baking powder, cocoa powder and salt, sieve over the egg and sugar mixture and carefully fold in.

3 Turn the batter into the springform pan and bake in the oven for about 40 minutes. Take out and Let cool.

4 Split the cooled cake once horizontally. Mix the cherry juice and kirsch, soak the two halves of the cake with the mixture and let stand for 15 minutes.

5 For the topping, chop the chocolate. Put the cream into a pan and bring to a boil. Simmer for 1–2 minutes, then add the chocolate, remove the pan from the heat and stir slowly until the chocolate has melted in the cream. Let cool slightly.

6 Spread half of the chocolate on the bottom section of the cake, replace the top and spread this with the rest of the chocolate. Cool completely, cut into pieces and serve.

CHOCOLATE COOKIES

Ingredients

For about 24 cookies

5 oz / 150 g butter

2/3 cup / 125 g cup sugar

1 tsp. vanilla extract

2 eggs

2½ cups / 250 g all-purpose (plain) flour

2 tsp. baking powder

2–3 tbsp. dark cocoa powder

4–6 tbsp. milk

¾–1 cup / 100–150 g confectioners' (icing) sugar, for dusting

Method

Prep and cook time: 40 min

1 Cream the butter with the sugar, vanilla extract and eggs until light and fluffy. Mix the flour with the cocoa and baking powder and stir into the mixture. Stir in the milk.

2 Preheat the oven to 400°F (200°C / gas mark 6). Line a cookie sheet with baking parchment.

3 For each cookie take 1 teaspoonful of the mixture and push it onto the cookie sheet with a second teaspoon. Leave plenty of room between the cookies, as they will double in size during baking.

4 Dust thickly with confectioners' sugar (icing sugar) and bake in the oven on the middle shelf for about 12 minutes. Let cool and serve.

COOKIES WITH CREAM AND CHOCOLATE

Ingredients

For about 20 cookies

10 oz / 300 g bittersweet (plain) cooking chocolate (70% cocoa solids)

3½ oz / 100 g butter, melted

3 eggs

1⅓ cups / 250 g sugar

¾–1 cup / 100 g all-purpose (plain) flour

1 tsp. baking powder

A pinch of salt

2–3 tbsp. ground hazelnuts

For the filling:

¾–1 cup / 200 ml heavy sour cream

¾ cup / 100 g confectioners' (icing) sugar

⅓–½ cup / 100 ml whipping cream

For the topping:

8 oz / 250 g gianduja (hazelnut chocolate)

1 tbsp. palm butter

Method

Prep and cook time: 1 h 15 min

1 Melt the chocolate with the butter in a bowl over a pan of hot water. Whisk the eggs and sugar until creamy. Mix the flour, baking powder and salt. Fold all these ingredients into the chocolate butter. Add the ground hazelnuts.

2 Preheat the oven to 350°F (180°C / gas mark 4).

3 Put teaspoonfuls of the mixture on a cookie sheet and make a slight indentation in the middle of each. Bake for about 8 minutes and then take out of the oven and let cool on a cake rack.

4 Beat the sour cream until smooth with half of the confectioners' (icing) sugar. Whip the cream until stiff with 1 teaspoon confectioners' sugar. Fold into the sour cream and sweeten with the rest of the confectioners' sugar if required. Put a blob of cream on top of each cookie. Chill.

5 Melt the gianduja with the palm butter, spread thinly over the cream and let cool. Serve with coffee.

CHOCOLATE LAYER PUDDING

Ingredients

For four tall desert glasses

For the dark chocolate pudding:

2 egg yolks

¼ cup / 40 g brown sugar, or more according to taste

3 tbsp. cornstarch (cornflour)

1¾ cup / 400 ml milk

7 oz / 200 g bittersweet (plain) cooking chocolate (70% cocoa solids)

1–4 tbsp. dark cocoa powder, as needed

For the white chocolate pudding:

Sugar, as needed

1 egg yolk

1 tsp. cornstarch (cornflour)

½ cup / 125 ml milk

3 oz / 75 g white cooking chocolate

To garnish:

White chocolate shavings

Method

Prep and cook time: 40 min

1 For the dark chocolate pudding, mix the egg yolk with the sugar. Mix the cornstarch with 2–4 tablespoons of milk and stir until smooth. Bring the remaining milk to a boil. Remove the milk from the heat. Stir the cornstarch-milk mixture into the boiled milk with a whisk, return to the heat and bring to a boil, stirring constantly stirring.

2 Add the chopped chocolate and stir until melted. Remove from the heat and blend with the egg yolks, stirring vigorously. If necessary, color further with cocoa powder.

3 For the white chocolate pudding, mix the egg yolk with sugar. Mix the cornstarch smoothly with 1–2 tablespoons of milk. Bring the rest of the milk to a boil, stir in the cornstarch and return to a boil. Melt the chopped chocolate in this mixture. Remove from the heat and blend with the egg yolk, stirring vigorously.

4 Fill the dessert glasses with the two puddings in layers; first divide half of the dark chocolate pudding between the glasses, and then add a layer using half of the vanilla pudding, then a few spoonfuls of the dark pudding. Layer the rest of the vanilla pudding next and finish with the remaining chocolate pudding.

5 Use a long narrow spoon handle to make patterns between the layers, by moving it up and down vertically at intervals around the glass.

6 Let cool and thicken well, garnish with white chocolate shavings.

HOT CHOCOLATE PUDDING WITH VANILLA ICE CREAM

Ingredients

For four 7-fl oz / 200-ml ramekins

For the pudding batter:

5 oz / 150 g bittersweet (plain) cooking chocolate (70% cocoa solids)

Scant ½ cup / 100 g butter

2 eggs

2 egg yolks

⅓ cup / 65 g sugar

2 tbsp. flour

Oil, to grease the ramekins

Sugar, to coat the ramekins

For the topping:

1½ oz / 40 g bittersweet (plain) cooking chocolate (70% cocoa solids)

1 tbsp. butter

4 scoops vanilla ice cream

Method

Prep and cook time: 50 min

1 Chop the chocolate into small pieces and melt with the butter in a bowl over a pan of hot water. Whisk the eggs, egg yolks and sugar together. Stir in the flour and the chocolate-butter mixture.

2 Preheated the oven to 350°F (175°C / gas mark 4). Oil 4 ramekins and sprinkle with sugar. Fill half full with the mixture.

3 Bake in the oven for about 15–20 minutes.

4 For the topping, heat the chocolate in a bowl over a pan of hot water, stir in the butter.

5 Remove the chocolate pudding from the oven, put one scoop of ice cream on top of each ramekin, add a little of the chocolate sauce and serve at once.

MOCHA CHEESECAKE

Ingredients

For an 11-inch / 28-cm springform pan

Butter or oil, to grease the pan

1 unwaxed lemon

Scang 1 cup / 200 g soft butter

1 cup / 200 g sugar

1 vanilla pod

4 eggs

3½ oz / 100 g milk chocolate (30% cocoa solids)

3 cups / 750 g low-fat quark or curd cheese

1 tbsp. cream of wheat

4½ tbsp. cornstarch

1½ tsp. vanilla flavoring

4 tbsp. dark cocoa powder

2 tbsp. instant espresso powder

1 egg

Method

Prep and cook time: 1 h 30 min

1 Preheat the oven to 425°F (220°C / gas mark 7). Line a baking pan with baking parchment and lightly grease the sides. Wash the lemon in hot water and rub dry. Grate the peel and squeeze the lemon.

2 Cream the butter and sugar until light and fluffy. Slit the vanilla bean open lengthways, scrape out the seeds and add to the creamed mixture. Separate the eggs. Add the egg yolks, lemon juice and grated peel and mix thoroughly.

3 Melt the chocolate in a bowl over a pan of hot water, then set aside and let cool. Stir in the quark, cream of wheat, cornstarch and vanilla flavoring. Mix with one third of the creamed mixture and add the cocoa powder and espresso powder.

4 Beat the egg whites until stiff and fold a quarter into the chocolate mixture. Fold the rest into the creamed mixture.

5 Spread the chocolate mixture in the prepared springform pan, reserving 4 tablespoons. Spread the creamed mixture on top. Put the rest of the chocolate mixture into a freezer bag and snip off one corner, then use it to pipe the chocolate mixture over the surface of the cheesecake. Marble the lines with a fork.

6 Bake in the oven for 30–35 minutes on the middle shelf, then reduce the temperature to 400°F / 200°C / gas mark 6 and bake for a further 20–25 minutes, covering with aluminium foil if the top is browning too quickly. Cool in the pan.

CHOCOLATE GATEAU

Ingredients

For 10 inch / 26 cm
springfrom pan

For the batter:

3 eggs

½ cup / 90 g sugar

¾ cup / 75 g flour

1 tbsp. cornstarch (cornflour)

2 tbsp. dark cocoa powder

1 tsp. baking powder

For the mango cream:

1¾ cup / 400 ml mango juice
(canned)

2½ tbsp. cornstarch (cornflour)

For the chocolate cream:

1 cup / 250 ml cream

9 oz / 150 g bitter chocolate,
60% cocoa solids

2 tsp vanilla extract

For the white cream:

2 oz / 50 g white chocolate

1 cup / 250 ml whipping cream

For the crepes:

1 egg

3–4 tbsp. flour

Scant ¼ cup / 50 ml milk

2 tbsp. melted butter

Water, as much as necessary

Butter, for baking

Method

Prep and cook time: 1 h 45 min plus 4 h 30
refrigeration

1 Preheat the oven to 350°F (175°C / gas mark 4).
Grease the pan. Separate the eggs and beat the egg
whites with half of the sugar. Whisk the egg yolks
with 3 tablespoons water and the rest of the sugar
until creamy. Mix the flour with the cornstarch,
cocoa and baking powder, sieve over the egg yolk
mixture, and then fold in. Fold in the beaten egg
whites and pour the batter into the pan. Bake for
about 20 mins. Remove from the oven and let cool.

2 For the mango cream, mix the juice with the
cornstarch and heat slowly, stirring. Bring to a boil
once, until the mixture thickens, then set aside and
let cool.

3 For the chocolate cream, heat the chocolate in a
bowl over a pan of hot water, then set aside and let
cool, stirring every now and then.

4 Whip the cream with the vanilla sugar until stiff
and fold into the still liquid chocolate. Put the cake

on a cake plate and place a cake ring around it. Put
the mango cream in the middle and spread towards
the sides, leaving 1 inch (2–3 cm) clear at the edge.
Put the chocolate cream on top of the mango cream
and spread right to the edge. Let cool for at least 30
minutes.

5 In the meantime, slowly melt the white
chocolate, set aside and let cool. Whip the cream
until stiff and fold into the white chocolate. Pour the
white cream over the cake and spread evenly right
to the edge. Let cool for at least 4 hours.

6 Mix all the crêpe ingredients to a smooth batter
and let stand for 20 minutes. If necessary, thin with
a little water.

7 Heat the oil in a large skillet and pour the batter
into the pan very thinly. Flip once, fry until golden,
set aside and let cool. Arrange the crêpe over the
cake, remove the cake ring, cut into slices and
serve.

DARK GANACHE CHOCOLATES

Ingredients
For around 40 chocolates

¾–1 cup / 200 ml whipping cream

8 oz / 250 g bittersweet (plain)
cooking chocolate (70% cocoa solids)

7 oz / 200 g milk chocolate
(30%, cocoa solids)

Scant ½ cup / 100 g butter

2 tbsp. instant espresso powder

For coating:

7 oz / 200 g milk chocolate
(30% cocoa solids)

5 oz / 150 g bittersweet (plain)
cooking chocolate (70% cocoa solids)

3 tbsp. palm butter

For decoration:

2/3 cup / 80 g confectioners'
(icing) sugar

About 2 tbsp. whipping cream

Method
Prep and cook time: 1 h, plus approx 2 h
chilling time

1 Put the cream into a pan and bring to a boil.
Stir in the chopped chocolate and let it melt in the
cream. Let cool slightly.

2 Cream the butter with the espresso powder until
light and fluffy and stir into the chocolate cream.
Chill for at least 1 hour.

3 Using a teaspoon, take 40 portions and form
into balls.

4 For the coating, chop the chocolate and melt
slowly with the palm butter in a bowl over a hot,
but not boiling pan of hot water. Set aside and cool
slightly, stirring.

5 Put the chocolates into the melted chocolate, one
at a time, and lift out again with a chocolate fork.
Drain and put on baking parchment to set.

6 For the decoration, mix the cream with the
confectioners' (icing) sugar to make a thick frosting
and pipe a swirl on each chocolate. Let dry and
keep in the refrigerator.

CHOCOLATE AND CHERRY SUNDAE

Ingredients

For four tall sundae glasses

For the chocolate layer:

1 cup / 250 ml milk

1 tbsp. cornstarch (cornflour)

3 oz / 80 g bittersweet (plain) cooking chocolate (70% cocoa solids)

1 egg yolk

1 tbsp. sugar

For the cherry layer:

24 oz / 680 g jar cherries in juice

2½ tbsp. cornstarch (cornflour)

2 tbsp. cherry liqueur

1 tbsp. sugar

For the topping:

6–8 chocolate cookies or 1 large chocolate cupcake

1/3–1/2 cup / 100 ml whipping cream

2 tbsp. cherry liqueur

4 tbsp. store-bought chocolate sauce

Method

Prep and cook time: 45 min plus 6 h refrigeration

1 For the chocolate layer mix the cornstarch with a little cold milk until smooth. Bring the remaining milk to a boil, and then add the cornstarch, stirring continually. Bring to the boil again. Remove from the heat, add the chocolate and stir until dissolved.

2 Whip the egg yolk with the sugar until creamy, then add to the milk and thicken over a low heat (do not boil), stirring gently. Divide the mixture between the glasses and let cool for 2–3 hours.

3 Meanwhile drain the cherries, catching the juice. Mix the cornstarch with a little cherry juice until smooth. Bring the remaining cherry juice to a boil, add the cornstarch, and bring to a boil stirring continuously. Stir in the cherries and the cherry liqueur and let cool. Reserve 4 cherries to use as decoration.

4 Pour the cherry layer on top of the chocolate layer and let cool for another 2 hours.

5 Crush the cookies or break the cupcake into small pieces and mix with the cherry liqueur. Whip the cream until stiff and mix 1/3–1/2 of it with the cookie (cupcake).

6 Put the cookie mix on top of the cherry layer. Put the remaining cream on the top, decorate each glass with a cherry and drizzle chocolate sauce over the top. Serve well chilled.

CHOCOLATE TART

Ingredients

For 10 inch / 26 cm tart pan

For the pastry:

2½ cups / 250 g all-purpose (plain) flour

Generous ½ cup / 125 g cold butter

3 tbsp. sugar

1 pinch salt

1 egg

Butter, to grease the pan

Flour, to coat the pan

For the filling:

Generous 1 cup / 250 g butter

7 oz / 200 g bittersweet (plain) cooking chocolate (70% cocoa solids)

6 eggs

1 tbsp. lemon juice

½ cup / 100 g sugar

Zest of 1 lemon

Seeds from a vanilla bean (pod)

2 tbsp. cornstarch (cornflour)

Method

Prep and cook time: 1 h 20 min plus 1 h 30 min refrigeration

1 Heap the flour on a work surface, mix with the sugar and salt and make a well in the middle. Chop the cold butter into small pieces, scatter around the inner sides of the well, break an egg into the middle and add about 2 tablespoons lukewarm water. Chop all these ingredients thoroughly with a knife until they resemble breadcrumbs. Quickly knead to a dough, form into a ball, wrap in plastic wrap and let rest in a cool place for about 30 minutes.

2 Preheat the oven to 350°F (180°C / gas mark 4). Grease the pan and coat with flour. Roll out the pastry between two layers of baking paper and use to line the oiled pan. Keep the pastry cool until the filling is ready.

3 Chop the butter and the chocolate and melt in a bowl over a pan of hot water, stirring. Separate the eggs. Beat the egg whites until stiff and add the lemon juice.

4 Beat the egg yolks with the sugar, lemon zest and vanilla seeds until foamy, and then slowly stir in the chocolate mixture.

5 Add the beaten egg whites to the chocolate mixture, sieve the cornstarch over and loosely fold in all the ingredients. Spread the mixture evenly in the pan.

6 Bake in the oven on the bottom shelf for about 45–50 minutes, until an inserted toothpick comes out clean, covering the top with foil if it browns too much. Remove from the oven, let cool in the pan for a while, then carefully remove from the pan.

CHOCOLATE HEART

Ingredients

For a 7-inch / 18-cm heart-shaped cake pan

For the cream filling:

7 oz / 200 g bittersweet (plain) cooking chocolate (70% cocoa solids)

1¹/₃ cups / 300 ml whipping cream

For the cake batter:

4 eggs

½ cup / 100 g sugar

¾ cup / 80 g all-purpose (plain) flour

1 tsp. cornstarch (cornflour)

2 tbsp. dark cocoa powder

1 tsp. baking powder

To decorate:

2 oz / 50 g bittersweet (plain) cooking chocolate (70% cocoa solids)

1 tbsp. palm butter

Cocoa powder

Method

Prep and cook time: 1 h 10 min plus 4 h refrigeration

1 Heat the cream, add the chopped chocolate and melt in the cream, then chill for several hours.

2 Preheat the oven to 350°F (175°C / gas mark 4). Line the heart-shaped pan with baking parchment.

3 For the cake batter, separate the eggs. Beat the egg yolks with half of the sugar until very creamy. Beat the egg whites with the rest of the sugar until stiff. Sieve the flour, cornstarch, cocoa and baking powder onto the egg yolk mixture, add the beaten egg whites and fold in all together.

4 Turn the batter into the lined cake pan and bake in the oven for about 30 minutes, until an inserted toothpick comes out clean.

5 Whip the chocolate cream filling until stiff. Turn the cake out of the baking pan, split twice horizontally and spread each layer with chocolate cream.

6 Reassemble the cake and dust the top layer with cocoa powder. Melt the chocolate with the palm butter in a bowl over a pan of hot water and decorate the top of the cake.

CHOCOLATE CHIP COOKIES

Ingredients

For about 20 cookies

Scant ½ cup / 100 g soft butter

¼ cup / 50 g sugar

½ cup / 100 g brown sugar

1 large egg

1 tsp. vanilla extract

Generous 1 cup / 130 g self-rising flour

½ cup / 100 g whole hazelnuts, ground

1 tbsp. cocoa powder

1 tsp. baking powder

5 oz / 150 g bittersweet (plain) cooking chocolate (70% cocoa solid)

Method

Prep and cook time: 40 min

1 Roughly chop the chocolate. Preheat the oven to 350°F (180°C / gas mark 4). Line a cookie sheet with baking parchment.

2 Cream the butter with the sugar and brown sugar until light and fluffy. Gradually beat in the egg and the vanilla extract. Mix the flour, nuts, cocoa powder and baking powder and stir in carefully. Fold in the chopped chocolate.

3 Put teaspoonfuls of the mixture on the cookie sheet, leaving about 2 inches (5 cm) between them.

4 Bake in the oven for 10–12 minutes. Let cool on the cookie sheet for 5 minutes, then take off and cool completely on a cake rack.

Published by Transatlantic Press

First published in 2010

Transatlantic Press
38 Copthorne Road, Croxley Green, Hertfordshire WD3 4AQ

© Transatlantic Press

Images and Recipes by StockFood © The Food Image Agency

Recipes selected by Aleksandra Malyska, StockFood

A catalogue record for this book is available from the British Library.

ISBN 978-1-907176-32-6

Printed in China